W9-CLD-414

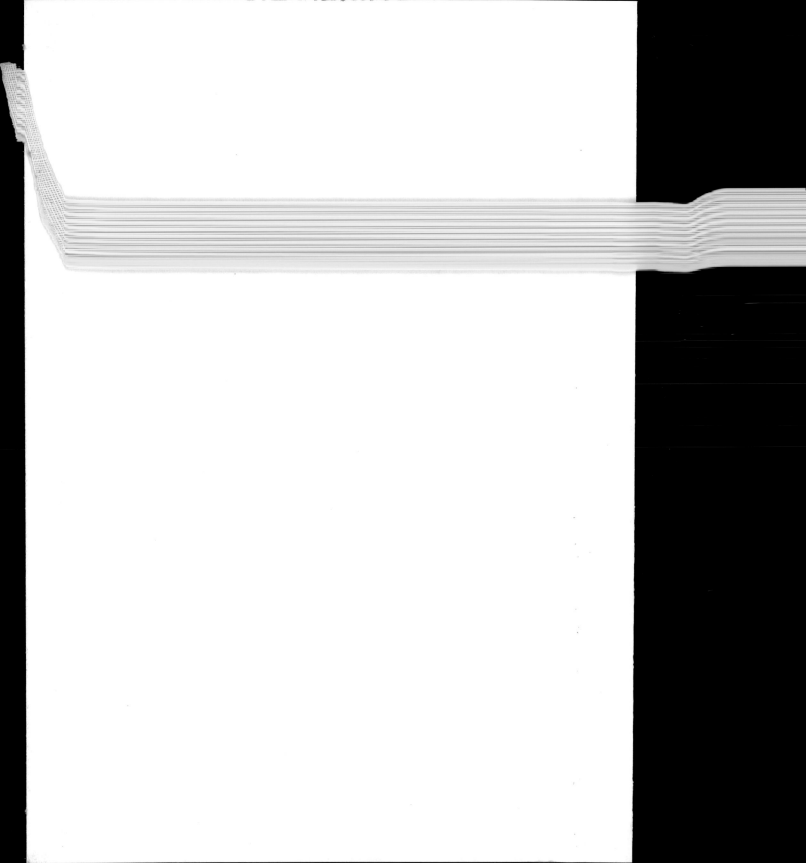

DESTINATION SPACE

THE APOLLO MISSIONS

by Patti Richards

FOCUS
READERS

FOCUS READERS

www.focusreaders.com

Focus Readers is distributed by North Star Editions:
sales@northstareditions.com | 888-417-0195

Produced for Focus Readers by Red Line Editorial.

Content Consultant: Dr. David A. Weintraub, Professor of Astronomy, Department of Physics & Astronomy, Vanderbilt University

Photographs ©: Neil A. Armstrong/JSC/NASA, cover, 1; NASA/picture-alliance/dpa/AP Images, 4–5; KSC/NASA, 7; JSC/NASA, 8–9, 10, 13, 16–17, 18, 20, 24–25, 27, 29, 31, 32–33, 36, 41, 42–43, 44; MSFC/NASA, 15, 23, 38–39; David R. Scott/JSC/NASA, 35

ISBN
978-1-63517-493-9 (hardcover)
978-1-63517-565-3 (paperback)
978-1-63517-709-1 (ebook pdf)
978-1-63517-637-7 (hosted ebook)

Library of Congress Control Number: 2017948047

Printed in the United States of America
Mankato, MN
November, 2017

ABOUT THE AUTHOR

Patti Richards is a writer, editor, and former teacher. She is the author of two books (*Snow Angels* and *All About Social Networking*) and several short stories featured in Amazon Rapids, *Highlights Magazine*, and *Boys' Quest*. Patti and her family live in southeast Michigan.

TABLE OF CONTENTS

CHAPTER 1

RACE TO THE MOON

A hush filled the room on May 25, 1961, as President John F. Kennedy stepped toward the microphone. Members of Congress listened as he gave a speech. Kennedy wanted the United States to send a person to the moon before the end of the 1960s. He asked Congress for the money to do this. He also said the United States needed a space program. It would be an important part of winning the **Cold War**.

President Kennedy's speech fueled the competition between the United States and the Soviet Union.

The race to the moon had started a few years earlier. In 1957, the Soviet Union sent *Sputnik 1* and *Sputnik 2* into space. They were the first human-made satellites to **orbit** Earth. In 1958, the National Aeronautics and Space Administration (NASA) was created. This organization would control US activity in space.

On April 12, 1961, **cosmonaut** Yuri Gagarin became the first person to orbit Earth. But the United States was not far behind. One month later, Alan Shepard became the first American to enter space. In February 1962, John Glenn became the first American to orbit Earth.

These early space flights were part of NASA's Project Mercury. Before sending astronauts to the moon, NASA had to develop equipment such as rockets and life-support systems. During Project Mercury, NASA practiced launching astronauts

John Glenn (left), Virgil "Gus" Grissom (center), and Alan Shepard (right) were part of the Project Mercury missions.

into orbit and studied how people could live and work in space.

Another set of missions known as Project Gemini helped NASA learn how longer flights affected astronauts. During these missions, NASA also practiced connecting two spaceships in space. Finally, NASA was ready to begin the Apollo missions to the moon.

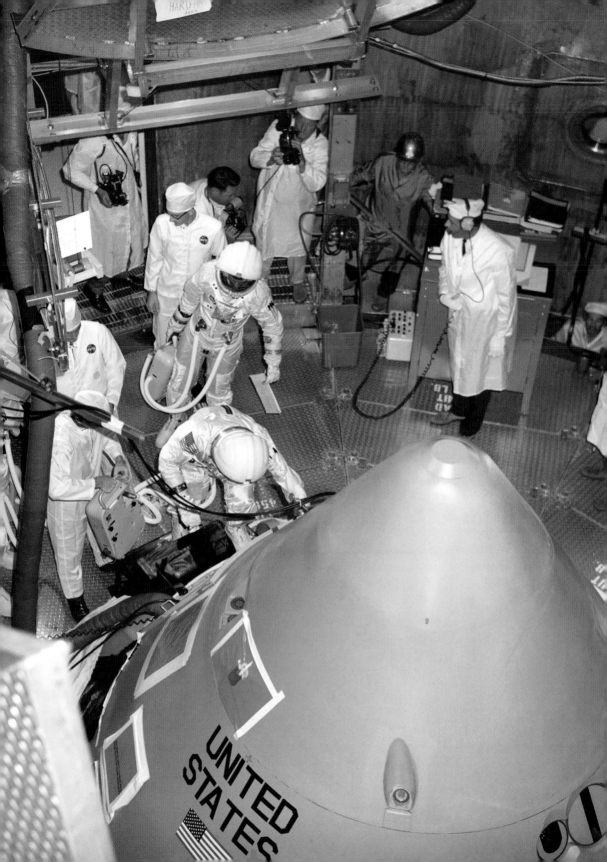

CHAPTER 2

ORBITAL MISSIONS

The first Apollo mission began in 1967. On January 27, three astronauts were strapped into the command module. This part of the spacecraft carried the crew and equipment into space. The astronauts planned to orbit Earth as part of a test. But during a launch test, the command module caught fire. All three astronauts died. Their names were Roger Chaffee, Virgil "Gus" Grissom, and Edward White.

Apollo 1 crew members enter the spacecraft's command module.

➤ APOLLO SPACECRAFT

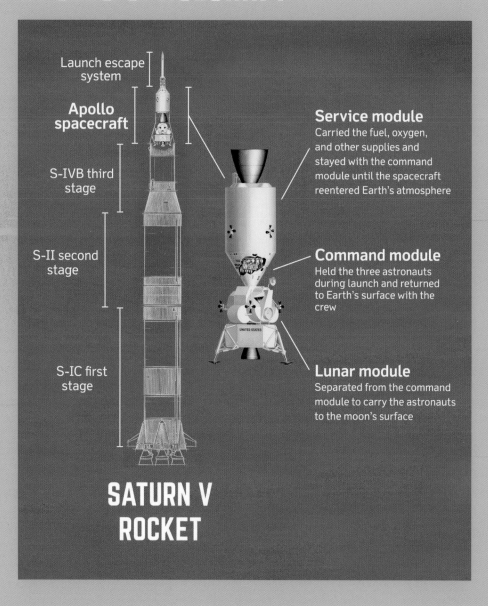

Launch escape
system

**Apollo
spacecraft**

S-IVB third
stage

S-II second
stage

S-IC first
stage

**SATURN V
ROCKET**

Service module
Carried the fuel, oxygen,
and other supplies and
stayed with the command
module until the spacecraft
reentered Earth's atmosphere

Command module
Held the three astronauts
during launch and returned
to Earth's surface with the
crew

Lunar module
Separated from the command
module to carry the astronauts
to the moon's surface

UNITED STATES

Before launching more astronauts into orbit, NASA needed to make the spacecraft safer. First, scientists and engineers had to design a better command module. During the next two missions, NASA worked to fix the problems that caused the fire. Both missions went well. The new command module was cleared for flight.

Next, NASA planned three unmanned missions to test the Saturn V rocket. The Saturn V was the most powerful rocket ever made. NASA used it to send Apollo spacecraft into space. Apollo 4 was the first launch of the Saturn V rocket. It went to space without a crew on November 9, 1967.

The Apollo 5 mission tested the new lunar module, too. The lunar module was a small spaceship. It would bring astronauts from the command module down to the moon's surface. Apollo 6 was the final test for the Saturn V rocket.

It was also the last mission with no crew. NASA was ready to send people to space once again.

Apollo 7 carried three astronauts to space in October 1968. This mission tested the service module. The service module gave power to the spacecraft. It also carried food and water for the crew. NASA wanted to see how well the command module and crew did their jobs. Walter Cunningham, Donn Eisele, and Walter Schirra Jr. took the first flight in the new command module. Every test went as planned.

Next, NASA would send astronauts to orbit the moon. The Apollo 8 mission launched later in 1968. Frank Borman, Jim Lovell, and Bill Anders became the first three astronauts to orbit the moon. During this mission, Anders took a picture of Earth as seen from the moon. This "earthrise" photo became famous.

▲ Bill Anders's "earthrise" photo was shown on TV around the world on Christmas Eve in 1968.

The next mission, Apollo 9, began in March 1969. During this mission, the astronauts tested how well the lunar module and the command module reconnected after separating for landing. After several tests, NASA was satisfied. It was time to land on the moon.

THE LUNAR MODULE

The lunar module had two sections. The ascent stage held the crew members. The descent stage contained the engines and fuel. It also had four landing legs. During the flight to the moon, the lunar module fit underneath the command module. Its landing legs were folded up. The lunar module pilot entered the lunar module and tested its systems to make sure everything was working.

When the spacecraft reached the moon's orbit, the lunar module disconnected from the command module. As the lunar module went down toward the moon, its landing legs came out. Then it touched down on the moon's surface. The astronauts stepped out and explored.

After the astronauts finished their work on the moon's surface, the lunar module took them back up to the command module. Then the lunar module reconnected to the command module.

▲ The lunar module could fly and navigate apart from the command module.

First, a probe at the top of the command module was inserted in the center of a cone-shaped device at the top of the lunar module. Then, three capture latches closed. After 12 more capture latches closed, the lunar module was fully **docked**. Once the astronauts were safely onboard the command module, the lunar module detached and fell away. The command module brought the astronauts back to Earth.

CHAPTER 3

MISSIONS TO THE MOON AND BACK

NASA used the Apollo 10 mission as a practice run for landing on the moon. This mission went through each step from launch to landing. But it never touched down on the moon's surface.

The rocket blasted off on May 18, 1969. It carried astronauts Thomas Stafford, John Young, and Eugene Cernan into space. Three days later, Apollo 10 reached the moon's orbit. Cernan and Stafford boarded the lunar module.

Apollo 10 launched from the Kennedy Space Center in Cape Canaveral, Florida.

⏶ Neil Armstrong (left), Michael Collins (center), and Buzz
Aldrin (right) made up the Apollo 11 crew.

They descended almost to the moon's surface, but
they did not touch down. The Apollo 10 mission
was a success. NASA was now ready to land
astronauts on the moon.

The Apollo 11 mission began on July 16, 1969.
A rocket launched astronauts Neil Armstrong,

Michael Collins, and Edwin "Buzz" Aldrin into space. After orbiting Earth 1.5 times, the spacecraft began heading toward the moon. During the journey, Armstrong and Aldrin put on their spacesuits and climbed through the connecting tunnel to the lunar module. There, they checked their equipment and sent video footage from the lunar module.

Three days later, on July 19, Apollo 11 began orbiting the moon. Armstrong and Aldrin entered the lunar module again the next day. They did one last check. Then the lunar module separated from the command module and began its descent.

Soon after, the lunar module touched down on the moon's surface. The door opened, and Armstrong stepped out. TV networks around the world broadcast his first steps as he walked on the moon's surface.

Buzz Aldrin also walked on the moon's surface during the Apollo 11 mission.

Millions of people back on Earth watched the historic event. This was the moment the world had been waiting for. A person had landed on the moon before the end of the decade. President Kennedy's dream had come true.

The race to the moon was over, but the discoveries were just beginning. NASA sent another crew to the moon as part of the Apollo 12 mission. These astronauts explored the moon's surface. They also took pictures of possible landing sites for future missions. In addition, the astronauts set up the first Apollo Lunar Surface Experiments Package (ALSEP). The ALSEP was a set of scientific instruments. It included a **magnetometer** and an **ion** detector. The ALSEP stayed on the moon when the crew returned to Earth. Its equipment recorded information about the moon.

THINK ABOUT IT ◄

Why would it be helpful to leave the ALSEP on the moon after the crew returned to Earth?

NEIL ARMSTRONG

Neil Armstrong was the commander of the Apollo 11 mission. He was born in Wapakoneta, Ohio, in 1930. Armstrong was a naval aviator from 1949 to 1952. In 1955, he joined the National Advisory Committee for Aeronautics (NACA). He spent the next several years learning all he could about space travel. His jobs at NACA included test pilot, engineer, astronaut, and administrator. After NACA became NASA, Armstrong worked as a research pilot for the Flight Research Center in California. He flew more than 200 kinds of jets, helicopters, gliders, and rockets.

Armstrong became an astronaut in 1962. During the Gemini 8 mission in 1966, he helped achieve the first successful docking of two vehicles in space.

After his first famous steps on the surface of the moon, Armstrong retired as an astronaut.

Neil Armstrong was known for his skills as a pilot.

He served for one year as the deputy associate administrator for aeronautics at NASA's headquarters in Washington, DC. Then he retired from NASA and became a professor. Armstrong taught aerospace engineering at the University of Cincinnati from 1971 to 1979. Throughout his life, he was given medals from 17 countries and received many honors.

CHAPTER 4

APOLLO 13

April 11, 1970, was a sunny day at Cape Canaveral. The Apollo 13 crew prepared for launch. Their mission was to explore the moon's Fra Mauro region. The rocket lifted off, bringing astronauts John Swigert, Fred Haise, and James Lovell into space. Five minutes and 30 seconds after liftoff, the astronauts felt something strange. But they thought it was just a vibration.

A Saturn V rocket launched the Apollo 13 spacecraft into space.

Once Apollo 13 made it into space, everything seemed fine. Other than some minor problems in the first few days, it looked like the Apollo 13 mission would be a smooth one.

A little less than 56 hours into the flight, the crew heard a sharp bang. A warning light came on. At that moment, the crew knew something was wrong in the service module. The bang they heard was an oxygen tank exploding. Electrical problems in the tank's fan caused the tank to overheat. When the tank exploded, the other oxygen tank began to leak. The spacecraft's fuel cells were damaged, too. The command module had lost its main supply of electricity, water, and oxygen.

The astronauts moved into action. The team of engineers and experts running the mission from the ground, known as mission control, searched

△ The explosion removed an entire panel of the service module.

for answers. The astronauts needed to leave the damaged command module. It had only 15 minutes of power remaining.

The astronauts floated through the tunnel to the lunar module. The lunar module was not built for long-term space travel. But the astronauts were 200,000 miles (321,869 km) from Earth.

They were still on their way to the moon. It would take them 90 hours to loop around the moon and return to Earth. But the lunar module was designed for only 45 hours of use.

Mission control told the crew to take the remaining power from the command module and turn off any systems they did not need. That would give them just enough power to return to Earth. But it would also mean turning off their navigation system, which was part of the command module.

The astronauts needed a plan to get back home safely. Mission control worked out when and

> **THINK ABOUT IT**

Why did the lunar module have such a limited amount of power and supplies?

⚴ Flight controllers at the Mission Control Center worked hard to bring the Apollo 13 spacecraft safely home.

how long to burn the lunar module's engines to produce the right **trajectory**. Then mission control calculated exactly when the crew should return to the command module.

Finally, mission control figured out how to safely power the command module back up. This plan would normally have taken three months to develop. But they did it in just three days.

The trip in the lunar module was challenging. The crew had little food or water. Plus, with its power and heat turned off, the command module got very cold. Moisture in the air condensed into water droplets. The walls and instruments were covered in drops of water. When the astronauts turned the power back on in the command module, rain began to fall inside the cabin.

One hour before they were scheduled to land, the crew returned to the command module. Their difficult journey was almost over. On April 17, 1970, they splashed down in the Pacific Ocean near the island of Samoa. The exhausted and hungry Apollo 13 crew had made it home safely.

The USS *Iwo Jima* lifted the Apollo 13 command module out of the ocean.

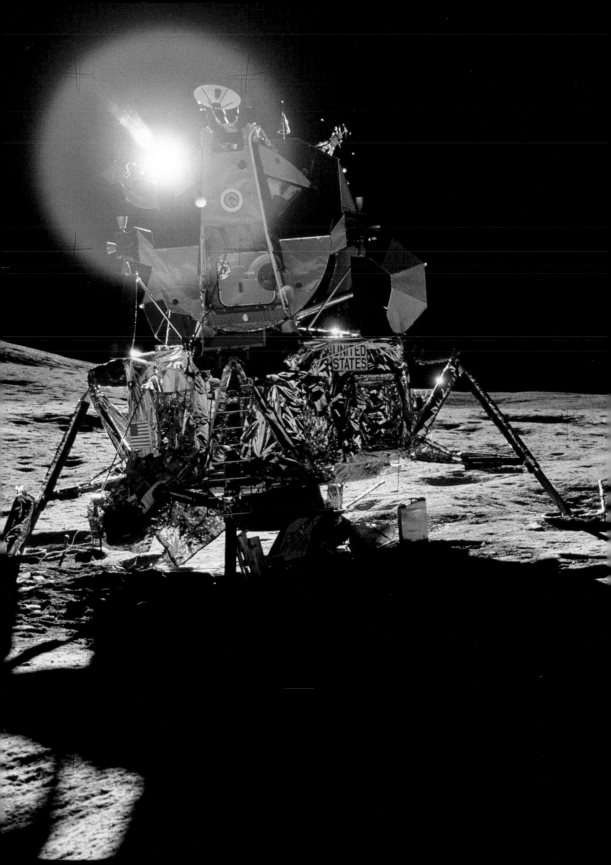

CHAPTER 5

RESEARCH ON THE MOON

The Apollo 13 crew had landed safely. But they had not been able to explore the moon's Fra Mauro region. The Apollo 14 mission would carry out that task instead. Alan Shepard, Stuart Roosa, and Edgar Mitchell made up the Apollo 14 crew.

Apollo 14 launched in January 1971. After landing on the moon, crew members collected surface materials to take back to Earth. They hoped to learn more about the moon's **geology**.

Apollo 14 astronauts took this photo of the sun's glare behind the lunar module.

They also took pictures of landing sites for future missions.

Apollo 14 was the first mission to use the new Modular Equipment Transporter (MET). The MET was a two-wheeled cart. It carried tools, cameras, and rock samples to and from the lunar module.

Launched in July 1971, Apollo 15 was the first mission to use the Lunar Roving Vehicle (LRV). The LRV made transporting equipment even easier. Because of this, the crew could collect more surface samples.

The crew also launched a satellite into orbit around the moon. This satellite collected data about the moon. It measured the moon's **mass**. Mass inside the moon is not distributed evenly. This uneven mass causes small differences in the effect of gravity from place to place on the moon's surface. The satellite measured these

James Irwin uses the LRV to explore the Hadley-Apennine landing site during the Apollo 15 mission.

gravitational variations. It also recorded how the moon's **magnetic field** and Earth's magnetic field interact. This information helped scientists understand the inside of the moon.

Next, Apollo 16 became the first mission to land near one of the moon's mountainous regions.

MOON LANDING SITES

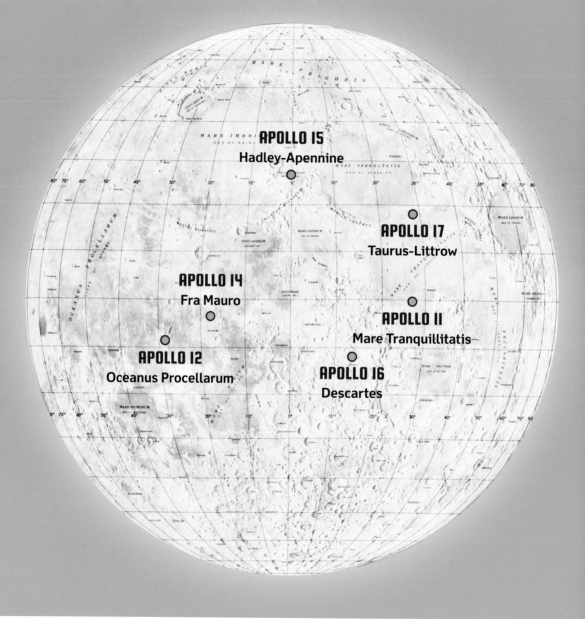

APOLLO 15
Hadley-Apennine

APOLLO 17
Taurus-Littrow

APOLLO 14
Fra Mauro

APOLLO 11
Mare Tranquillitatis

APOLLO 12
Oceanus Procellarum

APOLLO 16
Descartes

Launched in 1972, this mission studied surface features at a landing site called the Descartes region. This hilly area has long, deep ruts in its surface. NASA mission planners chose this location because they were interested in two volcanic areas at the site.

John Young, Charles Duke, and Thomas Ken Mattingly made up the Apollo 16 crew. The Apollo 16 mission lasted a total of 11 days, one hour, and 51 minutes. Young and Duke spent nearly three days on the surface of the moon. They did experiments and went on more than 20 hours of moon walks. Crew members also did in-flight experiments. They took photos while orbiting the moon and set up the fourth ALSEP station before returning to Earth. As a result of this mission, NASA learned much more about the moon's surface and geology.

CHAPTER 6

THE FINAL MISSION

After Apollo 11 made the first landing on the moon, the excitement of the Apollo program started to wear off. Many government workers and citizens around the United States believed the space race had been won. They thought it was time for NASA to focus on other goals. Others questioned the high cost of space travel. They thought the money should be used to take care of problems at home.

Astronauts stayed on the moon's surface for 75 hours during the Apollo 17 mission.

President Richard Nixon had wanted to cancel the rest of the Apollo missions after Apollo 15. But Caspar Weinberger, the government official in charge of where money was spent, convinced Nixon to let the last two missions take place.

Apollo 17 was the sixth and final mission to land on the moon. It left Earth and headed to the moon on December 7, 1972. Geologist Harrison "Jack" Schmitt joined Eugene Cernan and Ronald Evans to complete the final Apollo crew.

The Apollo 17 crew set up the sixth research station. They traveled nearly 19 miles (30 km) in the LRV. They also collected 243 pounds (110 kg) of materials and brought them back to Earth. These moon rocks are carefully stored and preserved at the Johnson Space Center in Houston, Texas. Scientists from all over the world study them to learn about the moon.

Jack Schmitt works at the Taurus-Littrow landing site.

CHAPTER 7

THE END OF APOLLO

The Apollo program lasted for nearly 10 years. It achieved much more than its goal of sending a person to the moon within a decade. During the Apollo missions, 30 astronauts traveled to the moon and back. Twelve of these astronauts even set foot on the moon. Now it was time for NASA to focus on other ways to explore space.

In 1975, the United States and the Soviet Union worked together on a cooperative mission.

An artist's illustration of the US spacecraft (left) and Soviet spacecraft (right) preparing to dock

⬧ Astronaut Thomas Stafford (top) and cosmonaut Aleksai Leonov (bottom) meet during the ASTP.

This mission was known as the Apollo-Soyuz Test Project (ASTP). On July 15, three astronauts were launched in an Apollo command module from the US space center in Florida. Meanwhile, a Soyuz capsule was launched in the Soviet Union. It carried two cosmonauts into space.

On July 17, the two space capsules reached the meeting point. The two ships docked, and their hatches were opened. The two crews met, exchanged gifts, and shared a meal.

The next day, both crews went back and forth between the two ships. They gave TV viewers tours of each vehicle. They also conducted science experiments. At the end of their two days together, the astronauts and cosmonauts exchanged their countries' flags. At the finish line of the space race, the two opposing teams crossed together.

THINK ABOUT IT ◄

Why do you think the astronauts and cosmonauts exchanged flags during the ASTP?

FOCUS ON
THE APOLLO MISSIONS

Write your answers on a separate piece of paper.

1. Write one sentence that describes the key ideas in Chapter 4.

2. If you had been an Apollo astronaut, which lunar landing mission would you have liked to go on? Why?

3. Which module gave power to the spacecraft and carried food and water for the mission?

     A. command module

     B. lunar module

     C. service module

4. Why did the Apollo 13 crew return to the command module before landing?

     A. The lunar module was too cold for the astronauts to continue using.

     B. The command module was the only module that could safely re-enter Earth's atmosphere.

     C. The service module was too damaged for the astronauts to enter it.

Answer key on page 48.

GLOSSARY

Cold War
A conflict of ideals between the United States and the Soviet Union that took place during the second half of the 1900s.

cosmonaut
An astronaut from the Soviet Union or Russia.

docked
Joined together while in space.

geology
The study of a planet or moon's physical structure, especially its layers of soil and rocks.

ion
An atom or group of atoms that carries a positive or negative charge.

magnetic field
The space around an object (such as a moon or planet) in which its magnetic force can be detected.

magnetometer
An instrument used to measure the magnetic field of an object.

mass
The amount of matter in an object.

orbit
To repeatedly follow a curved path around another object because of gravity.

trajectory
The direction an object takes when it is moving.

TO LEARN MORE

BOOKS

Hubbard, Ben. *Neil Armstrong and Getting to the Moon*. Chicago: Heinemann Raintree, 2016.

Morris, Neil. *Who Traveled to the Moon?* Chicago: Heinemann Library, 2014.

Thimmesh, Catherine. *Team Moon: How 400,000 People Landed Apollo 11 on the Moon*. Boston: Houghton Mifflin Harcourt, 2015.

NOTE TO EDUCATORS

Visit **www.focusreaders.com** to find lesson plans, activities, links, and other resources related to this title.

INDEX

Answer Key: 1. Answers will vary; **2.** Answers will vary; **3.** C; **4.** B